MEETING CHRIST OF CHRISTMAS:

A POET'S VIEW OF THE NATIVITY

SHERRIE MORRISON

ILLUSTRATIONS BY GUY E. SCAGGS

In Memory of My Grandmothers

These two women nurtured the love of music and poetry
in me from the time I was born.
I learned to sing acapella harmony from Dubby.
I memorized poems at Mama's knee.

Dovie Naomi Murdoch Hoover, *Dubby*,
my maternal grandmother
Fannie Bell Boughner Crawford, *Mama*,
my paternal grandmother

Guy Ervin Scaggs is an artist in his own right, having painted murals of an English garden, then a jungle complete with a treehouse bed, and finally a suite from Hogwarts in a bedroom of his home. Guy lives with his wife Laura Gail, his daughter Ellie, and two "like-family" young adults at home in Cayce, South Carolina. Guy is a proud grandpa as well. Brett and Chelsea Scaggs live nearby with their two-year-old daughter Evelyn. My request that he create interpretive sketches for ten of my poems has given Guy a chance to share both his art and his heart.

Camille Ussery, coached by her mother Renee, took the author's photograph. Camille began her adventure in the arts from a young age. Now sixteen, she danced in THE NUTCRACKER for eight seasons. Her musical talent, both as a soloist and in choirs, has been recognized. Her art has won high honors in church-sponsored Fine Art competitions. Her latest gift for "capturing just the right shot" is photography. Camille lives with her parents and two sisters in Columbia, South Carolina

Contents

Meeting Christ With Twenty-Twenty Vision

Christmas time comes once again and dominates the year.
It rolls around the circling years in faithful harmony
with the planets and the stars
while somehow the Christmas story has become a
marketing plan.
Or
The Christmas season brings pageantry and pomp –
candles and creches.
Is it possible that a clouded vision of eternity
Makes the birth of Jesus a story that only children believe?
After all, it is *an old, old story.*

Generations of two thousand years have arrived
and left this world.
Earth really is a terminal of sorts
where each person arrives by birth - situates for a lifetime
- and then dies.
Graves mark the departures as if life has no eternal value.
Yet
Walk the streets and listen. Watch the screens to see and hear.
The holy name of Jesus is shouted out in hate-filled curses
and with sneers.
The twenty-twenty vision of another life
has been polluted once again.
So
Come aside and meet Him. Make His name
sweet once again.
Meet the holy Christ of Christmas. - Jesus Christ - Emmanuel.
Set your eyes upon His kingdom now at Christmas
time again.

Matthew 6:24, John 18:36

A Barn, You Say

A barn, you say?   You've
got to be kidding!

A barn is no place for a
baby!

You're right.   Perish the
thought.

For Christ's sake, really.
Not a barn?

There's not enough Lysol
to kill all the germs.
    And… all that manure.
Yuck!

Spare me the details.
    No fresh air!   No soft
spots.

No, not a barn even – just
a cave.

Dirt   Dirt

What a tale told by firelight
(Chuckles)   before DHEC
took over health and
human services

So they piled up some hay
in a feeding trough. Right?
And…. what about

doctors and drugs? doctors and drugs?

We all know how filthy
such places are, housing
rodents

Surely the god who created | Surely the god who created
the universe
 did not plan story for us to
believe.

the universe
did not plan this story for
us to believe.

But then…

What other way would God
come to deliver a world
Lost in anger, lust, and
despair? (shrugs)

How could God get
holiness back into such
ranker and even attempt
to restore mankind to
Himself?

Wouldn't a kingly arrival
have called out the scribes
And Pharisees with their
quills and inkwells?

Absolutely! Each
"network" would spin
the birth according to the
political perspective of its
party.

Just look at what did
happen when Jesus
went public without
technology!

Just look at what did
happen when Jesus
went public without
technology!

Go back to that barn.   Can
you imagine the smell?

Cow poop?   Not fir trees
and peppermint? Whoever
wrote the Christmas story
must have got it wrong.

Obviously, this tale is for
the uneducated. Just look
at who came running in
this story of Christmas.

Sheep herders!

Sheep herders!

Let's go shopping!

Hi HO/ Hi HO
Off to the Mall we go
This is where Christmas is
found
      The Mall
RIGHT?

Hi HO/ Hi HO
Off to the Mall we go
This is where Christmas is
found…. Isn't it?
      The Mall!
RIGHT!   **Cut: It's a Take**

A Boy Child Is Born

Fresh straw fills a stable with soil's pungent scent.
Soft cries fill the air with new birth.
Tiny hands clutch the threads of a swaddling shawl.
Newborn eyes meet his mother's rapt gaze.

Mary's soft arms are the babe's resting place.
He suckles and sleeps at her breast.
Joseph's strong arms lift this child t'ward the skies.
Where the stars brightly shine through his tears.

Cattle and sheep low their quaint lullabies.
Herdsmen peek in through the door.
A boy child is cradled in old Bethlehem.
He is here in the flesh of us all.

His voice formed the orb upon which He now lies.
He spoke and all that is came to be.
Wisdom and Power belong solely to Him.
Now Christ's breath and God's breath are one.

Immortal mortality fused earth to Heaven.
God Himself came to us as a child.
At Christmas Christ Jesus brings hope and new life.
God knew this wild earth as a man.

Matthew 1-2, Luke 1-2

The term *immortal immortality is* borrowed from the play
THE MAN BORN TO BE KING by Dorothy L Sayers.

Perhaps We Should Weep At Christmas

Perhaps we should weep at Bethlehem
For here God came to conquer sin.
The lowing cattle in their stall
Could well be grieving mankind's fall.
For God Himself to come in flesh
Is not our modern Christmas creche.

Oh little town of Bethlehem
Your cattle cave held something grim.
The newborn king was born to be
A sacrificial lamb for me.
That manger in a lowly cave
Foretold my savior in a grave.

At Christmas when I see a cross,
I count my righteousness as dross
And weep to realize man's sin
Demands a savior for all men.
Only Christmas brings God near,
For God in flesh brings hope for fear.

A cave would be God's resting place
Until God's mighty power of grace
Would conquer death and set flesh free
To live reborn eternally.
From cattle stall to sepulcher
Christmas shouts, "God came to earth."

John 1:14

Why Celebrate Christmas

Why celebrate Christmas
when squalor frames the hearthstones for millions,
when iron fists strangle the subjects of tyrants,
when blood flows in neighborhoods riddled by war?

Why celebrate Christmas
when flotsam clogs waterways,
when bias gluts broadcast news,
when greed warps commerce?

Why celebrates Christmas
when selfishness separates families,
when loneliness haunts elder hostels,
when deceitfulness cripples nations?

Why celebrate Christmas
when jeers mock the faithful,
when snickers greet the noble,
when apathy squelches the passionate?

The prophets long foretold the answer.
The sages had heard, and they knew.
The Lord God would conquer this turmoil
through joining man's struggles on earth.

We celebrate Christmas
when convoys of hope feed the hungry,
when courts temper justice with virtue,
when citizens vote in their districts.

We celebrate Christmas
when volunteers clear roadsides of rubbish,
when newscasts extol heroes' mercies,
when corporate funds match selfless giving.

We celebrate Christmas
when fathers and mothers seek counsel,
when children share baked goods and carols,
when broken men kneel in repentance.

We celebrate Christmas
when cheers rise to honor true soldiers,
when leaders confer without rancor,
when blood, sweat, and tears rebuild ruins.
We celebrate grace freely given.
We celebrate love without bounds.
We celebrate God's divine promise
incarnate as man, though we fail.

I Corinthians 13

Two Caves

Oh, little town of Bethlehem
Your livestock cave held something grim.
The newborn King was born to be
A sacrificial lamb for me.
That manger in a lowly cave
Foretold my Savior in a grave.

Perhaps I should weep at Bethlehem.
For here God came to conquer sin.
The lowing cattle in their stall
Could have been grieving mankind's fall.
Christ's birthing, which was not so clean,
Sits, now, a spotless mantle scene.

At Christmas when I see the manger,
I sense once more earth's mortal danger.
At Christmas, God Himself stepped in
To conquer death's birthright for sin.
Yet there in Bethlehem that day
Was just a stall and some manger hay.

Born In a cave; born to die for man's sin.
Christ, the incarnate God, lay once again.
Then rising up from this place in the earth,
The Christ of Christmas brought mankind new birth.
Two caves: one with a manger, the other a tomb
Are places where God told the earth to make room.

So, come all you° earth dwellers weary of heart.
God used two caves to bring men a fresh start.
Come weep at Bethlehem, but weep tears of joy,
For great Truth and new Life came through this baby boy.
Weep for joy with the angels and let church bells ring.
For two caves hold the gospel of Jesus our King.

The cave is often either a symbol or a motif for the hidden, dark, forbidden places in the human heart. We allow hurtful attitudes to be born in the heart and stay there until the light of the love of God shines in and reveals what is in this "cave." Accepting Jesus as savior allows Him to enter into the dark cave of the heart and rise with "healing hope," and we are literally born again.   "Glory to God in the Highest, and peace on earth."

Mortality

You wrapped yourself in mortal flesh
To give us life eternal.
We live in death until the time
That mortal flesh returns to dust.

At Christmas time we celebrate
The coming of a promised king.
We live in hope until You come
For Christmas means a kingdom.

We live here trapped in mortal flesh
And celebrate with joyful cheer,
One day the Christmas here on earth
Will be immortal Heaven.

Isaiah 53: 5-12, Isaiah 61:1-2,

At Christmas

At Christmas, Heaven's gates swing wide,
And God himself bids, "Come inside."
Behold, a gift of priceless worth
Is wrapped in flesh and sent to earth.
Bedecked in swaddling clothes, He lies
Beneath a tree of stable ties.
Hark, an infant's cry rings sweet
While kings, low bowing at his feet,
Insist a star has led them there.

Proclaimed by prophets centuries long;
Announced to men with angels' song;
The Lord of earth comes from above
To bring to mankind Heaven's love.
Emmanuel, the King of Kings,
For sin sick souls salvation brings.
The gift of life eternal waits
While God Himself swings wide the gates.
At Christmas we are there.

Finding Christmas

The Christmas glitz and glitter that once brought such
gleeful cheer
Has lost it merchandising power in shopping malls this year.
Why clamor over Christmas lights and sleigh bells
in the snow
When thousands now face homelessness with nowhere
else to go.

While children's eyes still glow with awe at Santa's jolly face,
The frenzy of the adults' lives accelerates its pace.
We get our Christmas goodies from the stores right down
the street
And spray our homes with aerosols to imitate mincemeat.

The stores fill up at Halloween with Christmas gifts and toys
To prey upon the wishes of our little girls and boys.
We buy and buy to fill a void, and then we pay the debt
With anxious days and fretful nights called seasons of regret.

The wonder that was Christmas before man lost sight of God
Has been trampled into memories under mammon's
brutal rod.
Christmas was the time when God became a man on earth
Because He knew that our frail flesh would denigrate
man's worth.

What Christmas gives, man cannot buy with gold he has
in store,
For Christmas is the Son of God whom angels still adore.
If man would have the Christmas joy, then man must do
his part
By placing Jesus Christ back in a manger called the heart.

Mark 8:36

Christmas Light

Hushed - hushed and quiet
lay the town where
sheepfolds dotted shadowed fields.
Hushed and quiet -
Low bleating-broken
but hushed
Crisp - crisp and dark
ore spread the sky where
shops and shelters dappled ambered streets.
Crisp and dark -
Flickering lamp-illumined
but crisp
Worn - worn and anxious
turned the hours where
travelers crowded halls and taverns.
Worn and anxious -
Miraculous God-visited
but worn
Clear – clear and refulgent
reigned God's song where
heavenly choirs announced a holy birth.
Clear and refulgent -
Whole earth-trembling
but clear
Still - still and peaceful
slept the holy child as
love took on an earth-born human face.

Still and peaceful -
Powerful sin-conquering
but still
Blessed - blessed and redeemed
orbited the earth through
grace incarnate in a virgin birth.
Blessed and redeemed -
Woesome, sin-tormented
but blessed
Calm - calm and quiet
rest the hearts of them upon whom
heaven's Light has shone.
Calm and quiet -
Faithful spirit-strengthened
and calm

Matthew 1-2, Luke 1-2

The Word

"Let there be light."
Darkness fled.
    No corner of the universe escaped.
    There was light.

"Let there be…."
Suns, moons and stars coursed their orbits.
Meteors began their journeys across the heavens.
    Planets filled infinity.
    Shapes amassed in rocks and rivers.
Mountains and plains rumbled with creation.
Oceans washed shorelines in thunderous roarings.

"Let there be…."
    Tree roots dug their way into loam.
    Grass gathered in prairies of rustling green.
    Colors chose blossoms for their pallets.
Fish and all sea creatures made paths in the deep.
Chorales of birds and beasts joined the cacophony.

"Let there be…."
All that was not became,
    in an instant made of eons,
Time and Space replacing the void.

"Let there be…."
A human form rose from the dust.
Created in the image of the Word,
    in full measure, man began his keep.
Man's words – man's cries of pain and pleasure –
    proved raucous words of hatred, pride and greed.
    Then man's desires, twisted by his flesh,
spoke words that spiraled man downward into death.

"Let there be…."
    A virgin womb pulsed with life.
    The Word fleshed God as man.
A brilliant star appeared in the East.
Angelic choirs rehearsed a glorious new song.
    That which had no beginning and no end –
    pure, unchanging, life-giving –
The Word in human form lay cradled in a manger.

"Let there be light."
"…the Word became flesh and dwelt among us."
Darkness fled.
    No corner of the universe escaped.
    Creation's ancient plan had been fulfilled.
"In Him was life; and the life was the light of men."

Genesis 1-3 and The Gospel of John 1: 1-5

Now I Shall Give Thanks
for Christmas

Now I shall give thanks for the Christmas holidays.
What memories bubble up like festive lights to twinkle
in time -
memories of friends eating and talking -
memories of family laughing, kidding, just being together.

Waking up under mountains of covers to the aroma of
coffee and twitter of quiet laughter
Eating sweets with abandon for breakfast and never
checking a clock
Wearing a left-handed apron - keeping pace the bustle of
Christmas cooking and cleaning
Listening to hours of holiday music without commercials
and critical commentaries
Watching the sky parade of winter and waiting for the
wind to blow the wind chime buoy.
Beginning and ending a holy day with worship and
corporate prayer.

Christmas morning was a fairy tale –
a fairyland of packages spread around the feet of every guest.
Stockings belched bundles
of candies, soaps, sponges, mirrors, jewelry, notepads,
doodads.
Mother's pile paid tribute to her role as matriarch; she
began the festival of unwrapping.

Each one in turn became the honored guest –
Sarah Crawford, Sherrie Lynne,
Jim and Sarah Dilly, Ann and Bunny.
Three dogs joined in with yips and nuzzles.
Wrappings lay snipped and ripped,
OH's and Ah's   " Thank You, Thank You"
Around and around we unwrapped
for hours with breaks for cookies, cakes, and coffee.

Now I shall give you thanks for the Christmas holidays.
Your home with its gracious warmth,
filled to overflowing with a holiday spirit,
looked, felt, smelled, tasted, sounded
like a Hallmark Christmas card come to life.
When you remember all the Gramby Christmases past,
I do so hope you will join me in remembering this as one
of the best.

December 30, 2000 in my brother's home
Emsley Burdette Crawford: May 1, 1947 – December 19, 2001

The Angels Sang

Through His chambers bathed in splendor,
Through His corridors of time,
God the Father, Holy Spirit,
Breathed His breath of life sublime.

Once in time we stood on tiptoe.
Once in time we saw light beam.
God Omnipotent, Most Holy,
Breathed noon's fire from suns to stream.

We then watched in tiptoed wonder.
We then watched in fearsome awe.
God most Holy, God of Splendor.
Formed mankind and scribed his law.

Once again the LORD has spoken.
Once again His voice is heard.
God Almighty, Grand Creator,
Fills the heavens with His word.

Hark! Again, Our God is speaking.
Hark! Again, we hush to hear.
God Omniscient, Righteous, Holy,
Calls! His judgment must draw near.

Surely now He bids us downward.
Surely now in earth's black night
God, the captain of His army,
Rallies us descend and fight.

Will Our King not rank his legions?
Will our King not shout, "Be gone!"
God of purity and splendor
Will wreak vengeance from his throne!

In the realms beyond man's vision,
In the realms beyond earth's shore,
God, our banner, bold commander
Speeds us on with wrath full sore!

No?   A reverence streams from heaven.
No?   Soft stillness bathes the earth.
God of Light, Great Lord of Glory
Bids us go announce a birth.

Fear not! Fear not! Tell poor shepherds!
Fear not! Fear not! Announce joy!
God of Wonder now incarnate
Cries this night, an infant boy.

Gather, angels! Bring your trumpets!
Gather, angels far and wide!
God who rules o're all creation
Will this news our songs betide.

In the City of King David,
In the City Bethlehem,
God of Love, Pure God of Wonder
Smiles, while Mary cradles Him.

Now our hosts join with Heaven's herald.
Now our hosts choir all the skies.
God of Peace with heavenly radiance
Sleeps enthroned on feed trough ties.

Glory give your God in Heaven!
Glory give your King on earth!
God, your Savior , Lord Christ Jesus,
Born as man proclaims your worth.

In the realms beyond man's seeing
In the realms beyond man's view
God of justice, wrapped in mercy
Offers mankind life anew.

We who serve in ceaseless dancing,
We who serve through ceaseless days
God, the Alpha and Omega,
Join the angels' song in praise.

Luke 2: 8-15

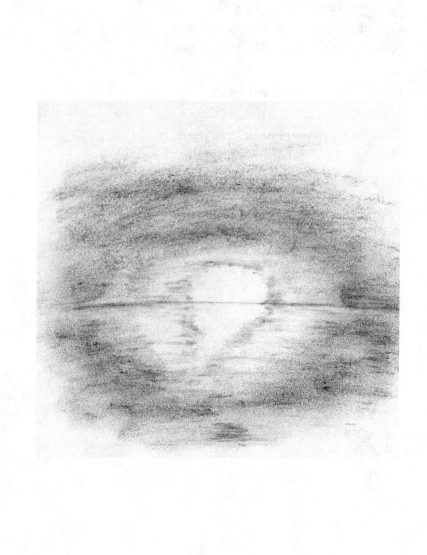

Forever Christmas

Before light broke through darkness
in a vast and fearsome void,
the God who knows no boundaries
designed His everlasting realm.
By His living Word alone
Love filled the universe.
God's plan and purpose for His work
displayed His majesty.
As Heaven and Earth twirled into space,
even then a Christmas carol
resounded forth around the Trinity.
Before mankind was formed and rose
from God's created dust and
God--breathed life began.
The glory of all Heaven's song
was sealed for Christmas Day.
Before clocks ticked the chimes of time,
a Love that knows no bounds
divinely ordained holy grace
with all of Christmas planned.
God knew that in His image,
man would choose to grieve His heart.
Thus knowing, God who gives all life,
prepared His Own Son's birth.
Incarnate as a man, in flesh,
God came as Love sublime.
Two thousand years – a blink in tears –
have passed since Jesus' birth.
yet, still unnumbered, faith--filled ones
share Christmas love on earth.

Romans 16: 24-27

Waiting for Christmas

Simeon, why do you sit so quietly by
Watching and waiting
In the halls of the temple?
Why, Simeon, do you cling so tenaciously
To the law, with your heart set
On Israel's consolation?
Tell us why, Simeon,
Why do you revere a hope
Your Messiah will come ere you die?
Simeon, Sir, standing here in this crowd,
You will surely not be the one
Who holds God's only begotten Son in your arms.
And you, Anna, dear, from Asher's line,
Do you think that your prayers will be answered?
Anna, sweet Anna, why spend all your years
Fasting and praying for Israel's peace?
Do you really think the Messiah will come
At some moment while you are here praying?
Will you weep for joy at the sight of your God
Snuggled close to a mother
And know then your vigil has ended?
How long have you waited and watched for Messiah?
How long have you both sought God's favor?
What kept your faith in God's promise of grace?

What was it like waiting for Christmas?

What was it like to hold Christ in your arms?
To know God's salvation had come!
How great was the joy having faith turn to sight?
To no longer be waiting for Christmas.
Two thousand years ago
God came to earth
And proved ancient prophets' words faithful.
There were those precious few
Who kept watch then,
Awaiting the Messiah's coming.
Where are you, Simeon, waiting again?
Where is an Anna now praying?
Who, in the years since the first Christmas birth
Hears Jesus' own prophetic question?
"When I return to establish my throne,
Will I find faith on the earth?"

Is anyone waiting for Christmas?

Matthew 25:25-28 and Luke 18:8b

Naught but Love

Look upon your gods and weep
at carnal treasures in a heap
of rubble scattered at our feet
and naught but fruitless labor.

See there in the setting sun
all the battles you have won
for lands and houses flaunting fun
and naught but endless labor.

Feel the endless sense of loss
knowing all you have is dross
from the fires lit by a cross
and naught but faithless favor.

Hear Christ's clarion call of love
divine mercy stirs above
through God's Spirit like a dove
while naught sans faith can savor.

Come now to a manger's seat
to kneel and faith-filled words repeat
as Jesus Christ you there will meet
and naught but God your Savior.

Stand and lift your voice in praise
following angels, eyes now raise
in Heaven's light behold Christ's gaze
and naught but life forever.

Isaiah 45: 15-18 The Messiah, God with us.
Pondering the scriptures confirming Jesus as Emmanuel.

God Came Close

Robed in placental splendor
The Lord of Hosts came down
His entrance without grandeur
God's brow without a crown

His throne, a father's shoulder
His banquet, mother's breast
His guard, dumb sheep and cattle
Man's flesh and bone, His crest

Two sounds ripped through night's darkness
One human, one divine
Co-mingled cries of childbirth
Announced God's grand design

The splendor of High Heaven
Abandoned for a stall
Where stench of shepherds' field robes
Filled censors in this hall

Though earth had been His footstool
He chose this wad in space
Deemed humankind as worthy
To shed abroad His grace

He left the realms of Glory
Bore squalor on this earth
The God of all creation
Came close in carnal birth

The Lord of Lords Omniscient
Through Christmas did His part
He took on my humanity
His destiny? My heart.

Psalm 8 (verse 4 in particular)
"What is man that Thou art mindful of him
and the son of man that Thou doest consider him."

Eternity's Author Is Born as Man's King.

Join Creation's Chorus
Sing Alleluia!
This day marks His coming.
Rejoice!
Be ye glad on the day of Christ's birth.

Sing, men of all nations;
join creation's chorus.
Shout!
Shout for joy.
Our God visited earth.

Though man does not hear it,
The mountains are singing.
Trees clap their hands,
and the oceans the same.
Every rock, every star, every created being
now has a reason to shout and proclaim.

God of the universe -
God of creation –
God of all knowledge –
The one God alone -
reached into time and in flesh sealed His promise.
His law is life, and His banner is love.

Oh, magnify Him,
morning star, gold sun rising.
Magnify Him, sunset rays on soft cloud.
Nature is lifting a chorus of colors
with music so sweet rising soundlessly loud.

Reds, gold, bright scarlet; deep, rich purple hue
create a cathedral with clouds as its pews.
Wild birds wing their praises and kiss evening skies.
Come!
Join the worship.
Look!
Open your eyes.

The sweet buds of springtime,
leaf-filled winds of fall,
white flurries of snowflakes
have answered God's call.

Oh, come let us worship.
With nature please sing.
Eternity's Author is born as man's King.

Isaiah 44: 21-23/49:13

Christ the Lamb

Christmas is the season
When we celebrate Christ's birth.
What we oft fail to remember
Is just why He came to earth.
His life would be fresh manna
Offered freely from above.
His death would buy our pardon
When we flee to Him in love.
With sacrament we see Him
In broken bread and wine.
Now the stable is a palace
Where His children kneel and dine.
This gift recalls the manger
Where our savior newborn lay.
This bread recalls the message
Christ, the lamb, was born this day.

Revelation 5: 6-14

The Power That Set The Worlds in Space

The Power that set the worlds in space
Came to this earth as man to dwell.
We saw God in an infant's face,
The Power that set the worlds in space.

The Power to conquer death through grace
Would one day break the bonds of Hell.
The Power that set the worlds in space
Came to this earth with us to dwell.

Come all you weary, tired, and worn.
Now at this Christmas time give praise,
For unto us a child is born.
Come all you weary, tired, and worn.

Let all the earth His name adorn.
With joy filled hearts our songs we raise.
Come all you weary, tired and worn.
Now at this Christmas time give praise.

Glad tidings spread through all the earth.
The Lord Christ Jesus rings new life.
All we who love Him know new birth.
Glad tidings spread through all the earth.

At Christmas we reclaim our worth.
Our Lord has come to end the strife.
Glad tidings spread through all the earth.
The Lord Christ Jesus rings new life.

The simplicity of the Christmas story actually captures the
awesome power of Almighty God.
In an attempt to capture this wondrous truth, I have
chosen a verse form that is most often considered a short,
witty children's poem. The triolet is in the family of the
"round" poem such as "Row, row, row our boat." It has a
nursery rhyme quality that juxtaposes the sublime.

In a Time Before Time

Christmas began in the time before Time
When darkness was darker than night.
The eternal almighty God only wise
Broke the void with His Word and breathed light.

In the realm of immortal and eternal Now,
Triune God in His counsel above
Knowing one day mankind would bow down to himself,
Set in motion His purpose of love.

In a universe filled with a God-inspired art,
Within the vast swirling He placed planet earth.
In all of creation, God displayed His power
Then breathed into man His own infinite worth.

Christmas began in the Time before sin
Turned life into death through man's choice.
The child Mary bore was God's Word veiled in flesh,
And in Christ men again heard God's voice.

This is the message that Christmas proclaims.
God Himself came and freed the enslaved.
The mission of Christmas proclaims this great joy.
Before there was Time, Jesus saved.

John 1:1
In the beginning was the Word, and the Word was with God

The Anointed One: The LORD Saves

Lament of Sight

Where is Christmas?
Point out to me what Christmas means
by what we see.

When science, law, and education
spurn this annual celebration,

TV ads and billboards flash
how and where to spend our cash.

Strip mall lots sprawl fat with cars,
their headlights dimming Heaven's stars.

Headphones, cell phones, iPod sights
mock silent, calm, and holy nights.

Liquor stores and slick cafes
line the shoppers' mad-some ways.

Where is Christmas?
Point out to me what Christmas means
by what I see.

Antiphony of Faith

Where is Christmas?
Here on earth Christmas means
God gives new birth.

When God Himself in flesh and bone
came to earth from Heaven's throne,

Entertainment, trade, and war
wasted hard-earned stock and store.

People traded, then as now,
birthrights for some sacred cow.

Children died from hunger pains
while rich men counted up their gains.

The leper, beggar, tramp, and thief
sought for solace and relief.

"Since I need," which God calls sin,
controlled the hearts and minds of men.

God had known since our creation
we would seal our own damnation.

Thus, before our time began
Christmas was God's perfect plan.

Christ, the Anointed One on high,
came with love we cannot buy.

Indwelling hearts of faithful men
Jesus, the Lord Saves. Amen.

Where is Christmas?
Here on earth Christmas means
our own rebirth.

Matthew 2:18-25

Bethlehem's Hills

Once David walked these hills then trod
by rugged men whose lives were hard.
This rocky, brush-strewn steep was home
to paschal sheep herdsmen must guard.
These shepherds watching their young lambs
Would not forget God's sacred words.
No spot, no wound could be allowed
on these most priceless, sacred herds.
Poor shepherds knew the flocks they watched
were set apart for holy feasts.
Drawn from their midst, unblemished lambs
would go before the temple priests.
Their bleating calls would drift away
to silence in these hills around
While shepherds kept their watchful ears
Attuned to rise at threatening sound.
The lamb-strewn hills grew darker still
while campfires waned and lost their glow.
The little town of Bethlehem
lay nestled near them down below.
What dread, what anguish must have been
aroused by angels' glorious song.
To hear a thunderous, Heavenly choir
and fear night's sacred vigil gone.
"Fear not…good tidings…" angels sang;
"for unto you a son is given."
"Great joy…peace on earth…" Could it be?
It was the blood of lambs bought heaven.

Prophetic words from Heaven's throne
announced to man a baby's birth.
God's glory, wrapped in swaddling clothes,
brought saving hope to men on earth.
God named him Jesus – God in flesh -
This holy babe, man's pascal lamb.
Shepherds would share His birthing hour
and worshipped Christ, the great I AM.

Luke 2:10:

Two Thousand Years Watching

For two thousand years, men watching and waiting
Two thousand years pleading, "Messiah, come"

For two thousand years peering into the past
Two thousand years seeking Christmas

Two thousand years of prophetic decrees
Two thousand years - then He came.

Christmas is coming, so be of good cheer.
Celebrate Christmas this time of the year.

Decorate trees. Set bright candles aglow.
Sing Christmas carols. Perhaps, wish it would snow.

Bake cookies. Wrap presents. Hang stockings with care.
Address Christmas cards for loved ones here and there.

Make merry!   Be joyful! For God came to earth.
At Christmas men celebrate Messiah's birth.

But, listen! Now watch! God's time is not known.
The first Christmas came. Now two centuries have flown.

Messiah, our Christ, foretold Christmas again.
Then the clouds will roll back, and a king will descend.

One day Christmas will come as a new celebration.
When Jesus returns for a king's coronation!

For two thousand years, men watching and waiting
Two thousand years knowing Christ will return.

For two thousand years, celebrating Christ's birth
Two thousand years knowing God came to earth.

For two thousand years since that first Christmas day
Two thousand years – Maranatha! LORD, come.

Isaiah 46:10, Luke 21:28, Thessalonians 5:2, Revelation 3:3

Christmas in a Time of War

A trough made for cow feed is where Jesus lay.
No wool for his comfort – just armloads of hay.

No doctors attended when Mary gave birth.
A carpenter's hands his first touch on the earth.

Strangers, not family, attended them there.
And smelly, poor sheepherders gathered to stare.

A children's tale, surely; this could not have been.
Should this be the way God would grapple with sin?

We all know in wartime the strategy's bold.
The worth of a victory is tallied in gold.

Man could not envision what God would employ.
His plan to rout death came to earth as a boy.

The years of his training were not at boot camp.
His muscles grew strong using wood lathe and clamp.

He studied the words of the prophets of old.
Their promise his teachings soon would unfold.

His hands worked in wood while his heart worked in prayer.
He headed for Jordan, the enemy's lair.

His own rough hands wiped away pain from blind eyes.
They broke bread and blessed it with power undisguised.

He challenged the lawmakers, humbled the proud.
No billboards were needed where love drew a crowd.

For this he was beaten? For this he was slain?
He brought us pure love, but we deemed him insane.

We mocked him and scourged him and spat in his face.
Then we nailed him to wood, crucified in disgrace.

While men sank to violence, Heaven's doors opened wide.
Now, all who seek Jesus are welcomed inside.

This Christmas comes splattered with turmoil – man's dross.
But look! There's a manger – a tool shed – a cross.

Eternity in a Day

Before light broke through darkness
In a vast and fearsome void,
The God who knows no boundaries
Designed His everlasting realm.
By His living Word alone, Love filled the universe.

God's plan and purpose for His work
Displayed His majesty.
As heavens and earth twirled into space,
Even then a Christmas chorus
Caroled forth around the Trinity.

Before mankind was formed from God's created dust
And god-breathed life began,
Christmas had begun.
Before a clock ticked off the chimes of time,
A Love that knows no boundaries
Had all of Christmas planned.

God knew that in His image,
Man would choose to grieve His heart.
Thus knowing, God who gives all life,
Prepared His Own Son's birth.

Incarnate as a man, in flesh,
He came as Love sublime.
Two thousand years – a blink of tears –
Have passed since Jesus' birth,
And still unnumbered faith-filled ones
Find love and peace on earth.

Romans 16:24-27

Wrapped in Swaddling Clothes

Wrapped in swaddling clothes He lay
in a manger filled with hay.
Angels sang His wondrous birth
while the Magi tracked His worth.
Shepherds came and knelt in awe
on a royal mat of straw.

How could this be so?
In that stable by God's plan
man's creator came as man.

Wrapped in flesh, the Godhead stood
In a workshop filled with wood.
Townsmen praised His craftsman's skill
while he served His father's will.
None could know that Mary's child
from His birth walked undefiled.

How could this be so?
In that stable by God's plan
man's creator came as man.

Wrapped in love the Savior walked
as with healing words He talked.
Throngs of hungry men were fed
with His words of living bread.
Blind men saw, and harlots wept
while the haughty skeptics slept.

How could this be so?
In that stable by God's plan
man's creator came as man.

Faith alone can show men more
than a simple stable door.
Faith has power to open wide
gates of doubt or fear or pride.
Faith is Christmas' holy call
to kneel beside a manger stall.

How could this be so?
In that stall on Christmas morn
Jesus Christ the LORD was born.

A Cattle Stall, a Carpenter's Bench, and a Cross

Chariot wheels rumbled on roads built by slaves.
Great ships plied the waves in their trade.
Soldiers kept order while priests chanted prayers.
And the masses worked on while kings played.

Rich men sought comforts. The poor sought their bread.
Both kept wheels of commerce full speed.
Crowds hawked their wares among gods in the squares
Where true godliness gave way to greed.

Joseph and Mary were dusty and tired.
They found a safe place crude and wild.
Angels kept vigil as Mary gave birth,
And a carpenter's arms held this child.

Carpenters' cottages do not house kings.
This common man's toil marked his life.
Here in God's favor a boy child was trained
To obey God in peace and in strife.

Thus, in a village with no public pride,
God took on the weight of a man.
Thirty years calloused the hands He designed
Working wood as He lived out His plan.

Thirty years carving and shaping His trees
Now foreshadow where He would be.
Furniture fashioned by cruel Roman skill
Held His flesh torn for you and for me.

Born in a cow stall, a carpenter trained,
God's Son brought His love down to earth.
Christmas reminds us that Jesus is Lord,
And His death brings men life and rebirth.

Come, all ye weary and wounded and worn.
Remember the carols and sing.
Sheepherders, scholars, and angelic hosts
Worship the manger-born carpenter king.

"Tell Me the Old, Old Story"
The Four Gospels: Matthew, Mark, Luke, John

Christmas Hope

An unseen hope awaits us,
Formed by unseen hands above.
An unseen power directs us
With omniscient, holy love.
Why grieve ye in the morning?
Why weep ye in the night?
Someday our souls will marvel
When we see His glorious might.
An unseen joy will fill us,
Poured earthward like a flood.
An unseen home will greet us,
Secured by Jesus' blood.
Some small gift tied with ribbon may
Look empty in men's eyes.
The unseen Lord to which it points
Makes it Christmas in disguise.

I Corinthians 2:9
II Corinthians 4:17-18

If Heaven Itself Could
Not Contain the Joy

How can we who know God now stand dumb?
    Do we not understand?
What fools are we to squander such a hope?
    Would we let rocks cry out while we plod on?

God Himself incarnate as a man has walked among us,
    Knows our toil – sweat-soaked and sore -
    Knows our cries of anguish at death's blow
        and has wept with us for broken vows and tortured
        strife.

God himself, eternal, Spirit-breathed,
akin to us now in our flesh through blood – yet fully God –
    For love's sake, joined Himself forever to frail earth
        by taking on our form.

Then, oh, then, what thunderous peels of joy
    swept through all Heaven and filled the universe with
    praise
        from angel choirs that sang of peace on earth.
"Good will toward men," they cried in rapturous voice –
    Good will and peace – what mystery – what wondrous
    thought.

His glory is made known in every wave that washes shore.
All trees respond in rustling choral verse to His broad
smile.
The clouds parade in rippling splendor for His pleasure.
Birds greet Him in the early morning light
where speres o color chime the eternal hours.
All creation moves to make Him known.

Dare we exalt the towers we have built?
Dare we stand dumbly here with stones' mute tongues
ignoring our Creator and His grace
when, for man's sake, He came to dwell on earth?

How is it we at Christmas chant of pelf
while all of Heaven and earth exalt Him on His throne?
Let praises flow and songs of joy arise.
Let worship lift our hearts before our King.
For Christ the Lord was born to set us free.
If Heaven could not contain the joy, dare we?

Psalm 96: 11-13

CPSIA information can be obtained
at www.ICGtesting.com
Printed in the USA
LVHW090352121220
673999LV00008B/171

9 781977 228857